SPECIAL EXHIBITION

OF ANCIENT CHINESE PAINTINGS.

INTRODUCTION.

The history of the art of all Eastern Asia centres about that of the Chinese Empire. Japan, Corea, Mongolia, Thibet, and, to a less extent, Nepaul, Turkistan, Burmah, Siam, and Tonquin, a great circle of neighboring nations, have, for centuries, drawn inspiration from the art and culture of the central power. Even upon India and Persia it would be possible to prove a strong Chinese reaction. Of an independent influence from India, it must be said that, though strong and special as regards the subjects of Buddhist art, it has had much less effect than the Chinese upon the form of that art in all these Asiatic countries. For them China occupies the place which Greek art did, at the time of Christ, for the many peoples grouped about the Mediterranean Sea.

Chinese art, even in its religious forms, has been preeminently the art of painting. In India on the southwest, and in Corea on the northeast, the finest specimens of Buddhist art took form in sculpture. But in China, after the sixth century at least, Chinese work finds its truest power in the art of the brush, of delineation, of inscription, of the blending of thought with the pictorial suggestions of nature. Primarily, it is the art of the harmony of the drawn line. It could thus represent in the days of its greatest faith many situations and feelings that lay beyond the reach of Buddhist expression elsewhere. Dramatic incidents, the relief of grouped figures against landscape backgrounds, the related idealisms of man and of nature, the imaginative suggestions of color, the atmosphere and clouding and light in transcendent aspects of the world and of heaven, — all these were open to it as never to the meagre severities of sculpture on stone façades.

The art of Japan, in many respects the most sensitive flower that sprang from this continental stem, combined the best traditions, both of Korean sculpture and of Chinese painting. But in painting it must be admitted that there have been few supreme forms in Japan which were not more strongly and simply used in earlier Chinese models. In the Tosa and Shijo schools we find the closest approximation to a purely national manner. But in Buddhist painting especially, the islanders closely followed continental influences. Thus a study of Chinese art is an essential introduction to the complete understanding of Japanese.

The earliest form of Chinese pictorial art which we can trace, and which belongs at least to the period from the second century before Christ to the fourth or fifth after, is secular in subject, depicting in outline or in silhouette the lives and doings of kings and their subjects, the portraits of great sages and statesmen, much as we find it carved on Assyrian reliefs or the walls of Egyptian temples.

From the fifth century onward, this secular art, bound up with the ideals of pure Confucianism, was for the most part supplanted by the æsthetic claims of the rapidly spreading Buddhist religion. The greatest Chinese masters of the sixth, seventh, and eighth centuries were painters of Buddhist altar-pieces, and decorators of the walls of large temples. The culmination of this art was at the

MUSEUM OF FINE ARTS,

BOSTON.

DEPARTMENT OF JAPANESE ART.

A Special Exhibition of Ancient Chinese Buddhist Paintings,

LENT BY

THE TEMPLE DAITOKUJI, OF KIOTO, JAPAN.

CATALOGUE.

BOSTON:

PRINTED FOR THE MUSEUM BY ALFRED MUDGE & SON,

No. 24 FRANKLIN STREET.

1894.

beginning of the eighth century, when the emperors of the Tang dynasty had extended their sovereignty nearly as far west as Arabia, and had established a system of administration, of competitive examinations, an eager scholarship, and simple, lofty ideals, such as become thereafter the crowning light and the central note of Chinese culture.

But a third great period of Chinese painting, that in which it rose to its culmination, was the glory of the Sung dynasty from the eleventh century to the thirteenth. This was the critical age of Chinese culture. It is not generally understood in the West that the greatest minds of Sung scholars, statesmen, poets, artists, priests, all were aiming to free their creative individuality from the deadening formulæ of Confucian tradition. All previous centuries are but preparatory to this suddenly awakening self-consciousness; all subsequent ones but a registry of the melancholy results of its final failure. But during its brief continuance it blossomed into a life of illumination, analogous to that of Athens under Pericles, and Florence under the Medici. For a moment all that is best and solid in Chinese tradition blends with the glow of Buddhist ideals, and with a new appreciation of individuality in man, and as reflected into nature. The key to this conception was a new philosophy which fused together the hitherto separate principles and cults of Confucianism, Taoism, and Buddhism, into a single new synthetic system of idealism, dominated by poetry and symbolism, which saw nature as the mirror of spirit, which prized individuality as the key of both character and creation, and which drove all the arts and sciences and codes of statesmanship abreast along a broad pathway of new experiment and of free reconstruction.

It was thus at this most genial period of Chinese culture

that Buddhism in its highest positive stimulating potency came nearest to the hearts of the people. It did so by enshrining itself within the temple of poetry, and amid the music of line and color. The bare abstraction of a heavenly harmony, which Confucius had asserted without interpretation, was ripened by it into a clear recognition of harmony as the life of the unfolding spirit. It is an oriental Hegelianism. It makes art the true type of life. It sees infinite analogy and symbol and co-operation throughout the kingdoms of created form. For it there is no abyss between man and nature, or between these two and the divine life of the saints. There is no subtle suggestion in the spring of tree forms, no massive or forbidding strength in rocky glens, no magic of the union between waterfalls and mists, which should not become to contemplation concrete categories of the spiritual life at which religion aims. For such transcendent conceptions the art of poetry alone would seem adequate; yet such is the flexibility and subtlety of oriental painting that it, too, dares invade this region on the wings of its iridescent color and buoyant line.

But within the church itself the most remarkable use of painting sprang from the conception and the needs of the so-called exoteric Buddhism. The difference between the southern exoteric and agnostic Buddhism, so frequently described, and the mystical evolutionary Church of the North, which has inspired the loftiest literature, statesmanship, and nature-appreciation through the whole East, is very great and real. The former dealt with man only, with a manhood that is to be feared and despised, with a salvation that is itself a negation of all values. The latter dealt with the undeveloped God latent in man, with society as a perfectible brotherhood, with nature as an equally significant product of divine spirit, with art as the expression of that hidden sympathy between nature and the soul, with worship as the organization of a life of perfect love and benevolence.

Whether the former be the primitive state of Buddhism, as some scholars assert, is rather a matter for historians than for the student of oriental culture. Their procedure would be analogous to that of an Asiatic student of Christianity who, having ascertained from meagre documents the condition of the Church in its first century, should thereupon disregard the wealth and power of its subsequent evolution, its part in European history, its capacity for adaptation to the infinite needs of humanity, as so much spurious perversion and accumulation. Christianity and Buddhism as well are all that they have become.

Two great schools of this lofty esoteric religion have existed in China and in Japan; one relying chiefly upon works and sacraments, the other upon contemplation. The former is still represented in Japan by the Tendai and Shingon sects. These preserve a ritual prescribed by superior intelligence as the key both to knowledge and to power. It aims at more than salvation, the human saintship of the Arhat, namely, at the estate of a Bodhisattwa, a transcendent love which desires self-development solely as a means to the whole world's salvation. The latter conceives of thought as the true solvent of things, and out of its potent depths would recrystallize the world. Its saints are Rakan, or Arhat, men who in the flesh by a life of this inner absorption have won power over nature, over the wills of men, and of the elemental world. For them the so-called magic is only an incident of the superior potency of thought. In spite of its benevolent use, a slight tinge of selfishness attaches to their contented isolation.

The paintings which are to be described in this catalogue were executed in this golden period of art for the Zen sect in China, whence they were brought by its pioneers to their first temples erected in Japan, wherein they have since remained. They represent the magical deeds of the great Rakan, in contemplation, in transfiguration, in their power over nature, animals, and men, in their benevolence even to denizens of the lower world, in their communication with the powers of the spiritual spheres, especially with the great Bodhisattwa. Thus we have here a most interesting record of what was contemporaneously believed of the mystical practices of these saints.

The subject of the Five Hundred Rakan, a favorite one in the Zen sect, is variously explained as referring to a group of apostles, who were the personal disciples of Buddha, or to the concourse of prelates who composed the first northern council, or as a fortuitous collocation of the typical deeds of Rakan, made under the influence of Chinese imagination. I am inclined to the latter view. Such pictures were used to hang about temple or lecture hall on special ceremonial occasions, either to stimulate the neophyte's aspiration toward Rakanship, or to increase the potency of his contemplative prayer.

This set of paintings has been attributed variously from early days in Japan, now to the pen of Zengetsu Daishi, now to the hand of Ririomin. The former, a celebrated priest, painter, and poet, lived at the end of the Tang dynasty in the tenth century. His style has more of individual strength than of ideal beauty, and belongs to one who is essentially a creator in a period of transition. That is one reason why I do not believe these paintings to date from his epoch. Also at that day there was no such rich treatment of landscape background as these suggest.

Ririomin, on the other hand, was one of the ripest and broadest characters in that most creative and individualistic period of Chinese history, the Sung dynasty. Though never a priest, and with all the knowledge and ideals of the typical Chinese gentleman behind him, he combines with these a reverence for and insight into esoteric Buddhism, which enable him to become the greatest pictorial exponent of its thought. He thus stands at the meeting point of the two currents in Chinese genius, and fuses into a single conception the wealth derived from both.

Though we are ignorant of the dates of Ririomin's birth and death, we can roughly conjecture that he lived from about 1050 to 1115 of our era. It is known that he took his master's degree in the year 1075, from which time to 1101 he discharged honorably his official duties at the Chinese court. For a long time he was reader and censor for all books offered for publication. During this interval he ranked high among the advanced thinkers of the age, being an intimate friend of the historian Shiba, the poet Toba, and the reformer Oanseki. His leisure he devoted to painting; and at first, like a true Chinese gentleman, he cared most for landscape, flowers, and horses. Also he loved to compose complete scenes from Chinese palace life. In the expression of character, emotion, and action, he was considered supreme. Later in life he studied the idealistic philosophy and mystic practices of Taoism. He also became intimate with Buddhist priests, who stimulated his imagination with the vast wealth of their spiritual conceptions, of whose splendors he determined to render himself the exponent. He studied the masterpieces of an earlier age, especially the incomparable Buddhist paintings by Godoshi, which were the crown of the Tang dynasty; but his previous training enabled him to contribute a knowledge of the fulness of nature, a power of expressive drawing, and a delicate play of colors under the effect of atmosphere, before unknown in religious art. In the year 1101, he retired to his mountain villa of Riominzan, "The Mountain of the Dragon's Brightness," which he had bought in the year 1078, and where now without interruption he devoted himself to the loftiest art. His real name was Hakuji, and his literary appellation Korin; but the title by which he is best known in history, Ririomin, or in modern mandarin, Li Lung Ming, was derived from that of his beloved retreat. Of his personal tastes we know something from contemporary record. The book "Hodenshu" says of him, "Whenever the weather was good, he went out with a flask of wine, and spent the day sitting on rocks, and calmly gazing at running streams." Guahin says, " He extended his hands widely to get hold of bells, urns, and other old altar utensils, with which he decorated his whole house."

The æsthetic character of Ririomin's work is perfection of style, a ripe mastery over elegance of line, an infinitely varying, unexpected spacing and massing, which remind us of nothing so much as the Phidian masterpieces. This quality of synthetic line is dominant in the work of his pupils and followers, and originates a school of Buddhist painting which lasts for a century, and then, passing over into Japan, is transmitted to the Takuma family. The question now arises, can we believe the present series to be from the hand of Ririomin himself? At first sight it appears that the pictures are not all by the same hand, and that they are unequal in merit. Also, in some, the composition appears to be finer than the execution. Especially in the backgrounds do we notice a falling off in power. Therefore, although we know that Ririomin did execute a series of the five hundred Rakan, we cannot believe it identical with this. Yet the conception, the color, the line, and the methods of expression are so close to those of the master, and are so characteristic of Sung work in the twelfth century, that we can be sure we have here a very important work of the Ririomin school. It is even possible that a few of the finest specimens are from his own hand, and it is probable that many others are founded upon his designs. We shall be within the limits of safety in regarding this series as made up of works by his followers, and executed at different times during the course of the twelfth century. A fading inscription in gold upon one of the pictures registers the fact that they were presented to a Chinese temple in memory of the ancestors of the Kio family in the year 1175. This has been considered the date of presentation merely; but, if my estimate be correct, it may well be that of the execution of some of the specimens. It is said that they were brought to Japan by a Chinese Zen priest in the year 1246. It is quite possible that gaps in the original series were filled at that time, as it is clear that later a few specimens of Ming work were added. It was in the thirteenth century that the first great Zen monasteries of Japan were founded, and the Zen pictorial school of Ririomin transmitted to the Takuma. These pictures were preserved in the temple Kenchoji of Kamakura; afterward at Sowunji of Odawara, whence they were removed by Hideyoshi in 1590 to Daitokuji in Kioto, where they have been treasured until the present year. This temple, now sadly in need of repair, has been permitted by the Japanese Government to dispose of these paintings, and has accepted the invitation of this museum to give them a first public exhibition to the western world.

Their general æsthetic characteristics are, first, a great variety and wealth in composition, each embodying an individual idea of line and mass unlike anything else in the realm of art; second, the more special line-beauty of drapery in the main groups which compose a subtle visual music; third, the fine oppositions of these to landscape backgrounds with their whirling, subordinate line-systems of tree and cloud; fourth, the richness and delicacy of their color-schemes cut by the cross-patches on the Buddhist gowns, and glowing from the low-toned silks like flowers. The remarkable degree of their preservation indicates the reverent care with which they have been kept. In few paintings of their age do we receive such perfect impressions of tone. Considering both their subject and their form, we may say that few such important remains of early Chinese art have been seen in the West, and, indeed, that few such exist anywhere. Of the series forty-four are hung in this exhibition.

ERNEST FRANCISCO FENOLLOSA,

Curator of the Department of Japanese Art.

CATALOGUE.

1. In this picture we have, probably, the introduction to
the whole series. We are, so to speak, set in the
midst of a domestic scene in Chinese life; while
the approach of the five Rakan through the clouds
above seems to bring the subject down to its nor-
mal connection with earth. The spectator is sup-
posed to be in the air with the Rakan, and with
them looking into the distant palace courts below.
In the nearer apartment, which is built out over a
lotus pond, we see a Buddhist priest officiating
with incense, standing before an improvised altar,
among whose furnishings flowers are the most
important feature. Back of the priest bend in
reverence two Chinese gentlemen, evidently heads
of the family, with whom are two ladies with
hands raised in prayer, and a nurse with a baby in
her arms. It is not unnatural to suppose this a
representation of the family of the donor of the
pictures, probably of the Kio family before men-
tioned. The apartment seems to be that of a
palace rather than a temple, and the gathering one
for the periodical worship of ancestors; but the
incident itself wonderfully illustrates that peculiar,
brief, and fertile period in Chinese history, when
all that was best in Chinese life blended with the
reverence of Buddhist ideals. Behind the ladies
and in front of a screen painted with a landscape,
two figures approach, one apparently a bearded

philosopher, who looks with some doubt upon the unusual ceremony which his younger companion explains. In the hall beyond, servants are preparing a feast on a long altar-like table set against the wall in front of elaborate paintings of the Rakan themselves. We may conjecture the significance of these paintings to be that the owner of the palace has constructed an apartment in which the spirits of the saints shall consider themselves ever the most welcome guests. The piety of this thought and the blending which it suggests between human family life and the full communion of the saints, is beautiful and significant. The faces of the real Rakan, who sweep to their hosts on the rapid clouds of thought, are strong and portrait-like.

2. Here are the five Rakan in relaxation; the three above sitting on a rock in a bamboo grove, the two below regarding the treasures of an itinerant Arab merchant. Of those seated, one holds in his hand tablets of scripture, another handles idly his rosary, and the third, like St. Francis, watches lovingly the flight of his "little brothers," the sparrows, among the winged bamboo leaves. The reposeful curves of this horizontally disposed group contrast with the fan-like spring of the straight bamboo stems, and with the vertical lines of the standing figures by which the feeling of the stems is prolonged below. To European consciousness, the upper half of the picture, with its fine relief of heads against the far-away river background, would seem complete; yet this artist has known how to weld the passage into a larger whole con-

sistent with the upright length of the picture.
This radical quality in the standing Rakan is intensified by the red, black, and luminous green of
their garments, which stand out against the quiet,
pearly tones of the robes above.

3. Those travellers in Japan who are familiar with the
legend of Benten, the dragon-goddess of the sea,
who haunts the cave at the foot of the promontory
of Enoshima, will be astonished to see this mystical treatment of a similar thought in an old Chinese
painting. Four of the Rakan, accompanied by a
Bodhisattwa and an elemental attendant, drift
across space in the heart of a fiery cloud, through
whose rifts are seen glimpses of the savage coast
with its blue-gray sky. From a cave in the perpendicular rock below them issues the flood of a
subterranean tide, tossing its freed fury into serpentine crests, amid whose commotion sits the
fifth Rakan in trance, like a sculptured pyramid,
on the outswept base of his flowing robes, dignified
as a Buddha, with deep breath, the body swaying
lightly backward, head thrown forward, hands
drooping in the lap like a flower; while against the
transcendent lines of its drapery plays the counterpoint of a great white serpent-god, who, rising
from the froth at the Rakan's side, leans lovingly
the bulk of his silvery body against the latter's
back, and, raising his neck in a fine curve, gazes
upward from lowered head into his master's placid
countenance. A soft halo behind the Rakan
softens the colors of the rock with its translucent
disc, which at once proves the Buddhahood immanent in the man, and, set in the very angle of the

cave roof, blends, what would otherwise be the
harshness of its lines, with the upper and the lower
groups. The sweep of drapery in the foremost
Rakan of the cloud, the deep purples and blacks
and stone blues which support the massive brown
head of the figure behind him, and the classic
poise of the figure with the elemental, strengthen
both in line and in color the supreme quality of
the transfigured Rakan, and render this picture
hardly short of the power and beauty of Ririomin
at his greatest.

4.   Here the Rakan are relieved in light against the gloom
of a wild glen. Four of this compactly balanced
group are engaged in special prayer, whose potency
brings from the hell of desire, a Preta, or hungry
spirit, whose emaciated form, breathing flame from
its mouth, bends in humble acceptance of the rice
which the central Rakan doles with a ladle from
his alms-bowl. Doubtless this is some great soul
worthy of such mystic favor, though temporarily
bound to the horrors of the purgatory where it expiates some sin of excess. The attention of those
in prayer seems riveted upon the bowl, as if the
rice, which slips through the Preta's gaunt fingers,
required for his use some dematerializing charm.
Behind the group stands the sweet figure of a boy
in a blue-black dress, who, leaning his head against
the rock, aids the harmonic rhythms of the chant by
tapping on a small golden bell. The amethyst
and chrysoprase and pale porphyry of the central
figure, passing into topaz yellow and the cherry fire
of opals, burn against the black masses of angular
rock, and the tall brown pine which seems to shoot

from its stony roots, like a rocket, to the top of
the picture, where it bursts into a shower of drooping, feathery branches, whence emerges one long
dragon-like arm to reach to the group below its
sympathetic aid. The play of mysterious cloud-
strata among the glint of these branches softens
their gloom; and the curving line of ragged rocks
at the bottom is, perhaps, the most conspicuous ex-
ample in art of the principle, that a total average
line-value may be realized in terms of details which
most conspicuously break it.

5. The subject of this painting is one of the most interesting in the series. The upper group of figures
consists of four Rakan standing in the robes of full
priesthood, and of the fifth who has seated himself
upon a green throne inlaid with gold lotus, and
placed in the corridor of a temple whose pillars and
railing are seen behind. There transfigured, he
has pulled aside the bronze skin of his face, as if
it were a mask, and revealed beneath the luminous
features of the eleven-headed Kwannon. Within
the Rakan this highest of the Bodhisattwa has
been temporarily incarnated. The figure in front,
holding a golden censer in the act of worship, appears to be a Chinese prince robed as a priest.
The figure in black behind him is that of an ordinary priest in prayer. The two men in the foreground, apparently Chinese philosophers or scholars,
who hold in their hands an outline portrait of the
Rakan which they have drawn, seem now to turn
away from his manifestation in wonder or in scep-
ticism. The small boy in front holds an inkstand.
Behind, the water-worn rock of lapis-lazuli and

the bamboo grove are characteristic of Chinese gardens. The play of cloud through all parts of the picture, as in many others of the series, is an accompaniment of the supernatural act, and also serves to blend the masses of the composition. Aesthetically the greatest quality of the painting is an undulating, aspiring, flame-like system of lines, which, rooted in the angular, grayish, human masses in the lower left corner, courses along the line of the censer, swells through the living curves of the Bodhisattwa's raiment, and whirls into the emerald and ruby of the upper Rakan, where it meets the lapping tongues of the descending clouds. The vertical lines of the vermilion columns, though broken, seem to hold this upward motion as in a frame. The drawing and the characterization of the scholars, especially in the heads, is not unworthy of a Holbein, or a Dürer, and suggests the power of Chinese portrait painting at its ripest.

6. The dramatic incident is here patent; the transfiguration of one of the five swept up from the wildness of earthy tree and cloud into the soft descending clouds of heaven, where the very lines of his gauzy drapery seem to be lengthened into curves of supernatural beauty, while from his head issues a slight spray of a spiritual substance like water, which separating into two streams, follows the divine grace and benignity of movement of the hands, near which they break into the air in fingers of spray. The angularity and rough curvature of the figures on earth, the strength of drawing in the rocks, and especially in the gnarled tree, the leap of the waterfall, the fine preservation of the lower

part of the picture, and the jewel-like intrusion of
the two small passages of red, enter notably into
the striking originality and impression of this
work.

7. This represents the five Rakan crossing a turbulent
   stream, — one upon a reed, one upon his straw hat,
   one upon a black cloak, one upon his staff, and the
   fifth upon a tree trunk. A strong wind playing on
   the sails of their ample garments drives them
   along through a moving medium of mingled cloud
   and sea, and twists up the folds and patches of
   their draperies into knotted and snaky line systems,
   which open the eye to the possibility of violent
   rhythms as pure and individual and creative as
   those we have learned to understand in the repose of classic sculpture. It is a new species of
   pictorial idea. Only the upper Rakan stands un-
   moved amid the tossing masses of the picture, as
   if he accompanied the others, rather through the
   benignity of his calm contemplation, than by the
   impact of any terrestrial motor. His color, too,
   is like an opalescent dream ; and the soft grays
   of the three below, shot with lightning jags of
   black, serve to throw up into jewel-like intensity,
   the reds and greens of the lower figure.

8. Though lacking the solidity of composition, and the
   grace and peace of the preceding pictures, this
   realizes a pictorial idea no less clear and strong.
   The amorphous rock masses, and the pre-diluvian
   tree seem like splinters from some primeval world,
   and from its iron coils human figures emerge, as
   life from chaos. The cleft in the centre, where

boils a torrent, is as if rent by recent earthquake; and the angular unsoftened lines of the garments hold their place among the rugged surroundings, and contrast with the delicate feminine curves of the Tennin, or angel, who descends bearing a dish of heavenly flowers to their forbidding sphere, in the folds of a soft mauve cloud. The unconventional, nervously drawn whirls of this cloud, even in its softest portions, is a supreme model for the world's designers. There is nothing in Western art to compare with the dragon-like trunk of the almost leafless tree. The figure with red-brown flesh behind it is a Ten or Deva, belonging, like the angel, to the world of higher elemental spirits.

9. Here is another group of the Rakan in repose, watching an Arab trader who presents, in a shallow bowl, a tree of coral, which seems to become alive with rosy buds at the ends of its branches. Such a light miracle, though it attracts the attention of all, seems to be easily performed by the single Rakan who prays with one hand on his beads. The fine figure of a servant behind brings in a bundle of Scripture rolls, wrapped in a bamboo covering. To the left of the trader is his beast of burden. Above, we have a magnificent wild tree blending with an equally wild sky. The sombre coloring of the garments in which no red occurs and the rich tones of the landscape are noticeable in this work.

10. In this picture the Rakan are grouped about the rocky pathway to a Buddhist temple, near the pillar of which stands the figure of a Deva. The

sistent with the upright length of the picture. This radical quality in the standing Rakan is intensified by the red, black, and luminous green of their garments, which stand out against the quiet, pearly tones of the robes above.

3. Those travellers in Japan who are familiar with the legend of Benten, the dragon-goddess of the sea, who haunts the cave at the foot of the promontory of Enoshima, will be astonished to see this mystical treatment of a similar thought in an old Chinese painting. Four of the Rakan, accompanied by a Bodhisattwa and an elemental attendant, drift across space in the heart of a fiery cloud, through whose rifts are seen glimpses of the savage coast with its blue-gray sky. From a cave in the perpendicular rock below them issues the flood of a subterranean tide, tossing its freed fury into serpentine crests, amid whose commotion sits the fifth Rakan in trance, like a sculptured pyramid, on the outswept base of his flowing robes, dignified as a Buddha, with deep breath, the body swaying lightly backward, head thrown forward, hands drooping in the lap like a flower; while against the transcendent lines of its drapery plays the counterpoint of a great white serpent-god, who, rising from the froth at the Rakan's side, leans lovingly the bulk of his silvery body against the latter's back, and, raising his neck in a fine curve, gazes upward from lowered head into his master's placid countenance. A soft halo behind the Rakan softens the colors of the rock with its translucent disc, which at once proves the Buddhahood immanent in the man, and, set in the very angle of the

cave roof, blends, what would otherwise be the harshness of its lines, with the upper and the lower groups. The sweep of drapery in the foremost Rakan of the cloud, the deep purples and blacks and stone blues which support the massive brown head of the figure behind him, and the classic poise of the figure with the elemental, strengthen both in line and in color the supreme quality of the transfigured Rakan, and render this picture hardly short of the power and beauty of Ririomin at his greatest.

4.   Here the Rakan are relieved in light against the gloom of a wild glen. Four of this compactly balanced group are engaged in special prayer, whose potency brings from the hell of desire, a Preta, or hungry spirit, whose emaciated form, breathing flame from its mouth, bends in humble acceptance of the rice which the central Rakan doles with a ladle from his alms-bowl. Doubtless this is some great soul worthy of such mystic favor, though temporarily bound to the horrors of the purgatory where it expiates some sin of excess. The attention of those in prayer seems riveted upon the bowl, as if the rice, which slips through the Preta's gaunt fingers, required for his use some dematerializing charm. Behind the group stands the sweet figure of a boy in a blue-black dress, who, leaning his head against the rock, aids the harmonic rhythms of the chant by tapping on a small golden bell. The amethyst and chrysoprase and pale porphyry of the central figure, passing into topaz yellow and the cherry fire of opals, burn against the black masses of angular rock, and the tall brown pine which seems to shoot

from its stony roots, like a rocket, to the top of
the picture, where it bursts into a shower of drooping, feathery branches, whence emerges one long
dragon-like arm to reach to the group below its
sympathetic aid. The play of mysterious cloud-
strata among the glint of these branches softens
their gloom; and the curving line of ragged rocks
at the bottom is, perhaps, the most conspicuous ex-
ample in art of the principle, that a total average
line-value may be realized in terms of details which
most conspicuously break it.

5. The subject of this painting is one of the most interesting in the series. The upper group of figures
consists of four Rakan standing in the robes of full
priesthood, and of the fifth who has seated himself
upon a green throne inlaid with gold lotus, and
placed in the corridor of a temple whose pillars and
railing are seen behind. There transfigured, he
has pulled aside the bronze skin of his face, as if
it were a mask, and revealed beneath the luminous
features of the eleven-headed Kwannon. Within
the Rakan this highest of the Bodhisattwa has
been temporarily incarnated. The figure in front,
holding a golden censer in the act of worship, appears to be a Chinese prince robed as a priest.
The figure in black behind him is that of an ordinary priest in prayer. The two men in the foreground, apparently Chinese philosophers or scholars,
who hold in their hands an outline portrait of the
Rakan which they have drawn, seem now to turn
away from his manifestation in wonder or in scep-
ticism. The small boy in front holds an inkstand.
Behind, the water-worn rock of lapis-lazuli and

the bamboo grove are characteristic of Chinese gardens. The play of cloud through all parts of the picture, as in many others of the series, is an accompaniment of the supernatural act, and also serves to blend the masses of the composition. Aesthetically the greatest quality of the painting is an undulating, aspiring, flame-like system of lines, which, rooted in the angular, grayish, human masses in the lower left corner, courses along the line of the censer, swells through the living curves of the Bodhisattwa's raiment, and whirls into the emerald and ruby of the upper Rakan, where it meets the lapping tongues of the descending clouds. The vertical lines of the vermilion columns, though broken, seem to hold this upward motion as in a frame. The drawing and the characterization of the scholars, especially in the heads, is not unworthy of a Holbein, or a Dürer, and suggests the power of Chinese portrait painting at its ripest.

6. The dramatic incident is here patent ; the transfiguration of one of the five swept up from the wildness of earthy tree and cloud into the soft descending clouds of heaven, where the very lines of his gauzy drapery seem to be lengthened into curves of supernatural beauty, while from his head issues a slight spray of a spiritual substance like water, which separating into two streams, follows the divine grace and benignity of movement of the hands, near which they break into the air in fingers of spray. The angularity and rough curvature of the figures on earth, the strength of drawing in the rocks, and especially in the gnarled tree, the leap of the waterfall, the fine preservation of the lower

dhism, of crypts and caves deep in the recesses of sacred mountains, where the Holy of Holies is unveiled to the eyes of the masters. Here an altar in three tiers of stone has been raised, and upon it has been deposited a bundle of scrolls, doubtless scripture, and probably believed to be some holy original of Buddha's date. About it, in the attitude of prayer, stand the Rakan who have brought to the mystic rite five Chinese laymen. In this solemn cave is performed the miracle of fire's descending upon the books, which, so far from being consumed, shed pencils of rainbow rays out to all space. The simple, unaffected grouping adds to the impressiveness. One can feel the all-conquering force that radiates from the altar, fills the cave, and drives into its furthest corner, in a bewildering group, the unprepared laymen. The figure of one who throws himself backward toward the spectator, in a frenzy of adoration, is especially striking.

18. Five Rakan, borne through the air on beautiful blue clouds, look down upon an Arab merchant riding on a heavily laden camel. The landscape background is mostly eaten away; but we can still see how the two groups were held together by the soft fingers of the cloud, and the fiery threads of the coral mass which the merchant holds. The coloring of the Rakan is unusually deep and startling in its contrasts; the group of the one in pink and green, and of the one with the dark head relieved against the former, composing almost the finest single passage in the whole series.

19. The Rakan seem to twine themselves about the
trunk of a gnarled tree in a mountain chasm,
through whose gap breaks a distant view of lake
and waterfall.   But the extraordinary thing is the
quality of the atmosphere, clear and deep, shot
with spirally ascending clouds, and cut with bands
of light-like paths traversing all space, upon
which are hurrying winged bat-like elemental
spirits as messengers, carrying in their hands
each a casket.   One of these lines descends and
ends with the group of the Rakan.   The beauty
of this mystical suggestion of space and cloud
and magnetic ray is startling ; but it is a revela-
tion to see represented in Chinese painting, eight
hundred years old, a recognized fact of mystic in-
tercommunication in a manner much like that
asserted so positively by modern theosophists
and actually claimed as visible by clairvoyants.

20. Sitting before this miracle, and forgetting the grand-
eur of those that have preceded, it seems for the
moment to surpass all previous conceptions of
religious beauty and sublimity.   Four of the
Rakan, with two Deva attendants, stand at the
bottom in symmetrical groups of three.   The
central Rakan has been lifted into space on an
altar of two confluent blue clouds, where he sits
cross-legged as a calm Buddha against a palpi-
tating background of blue fire, into which other
tongues of the paler cloud lap from either side.
An enormous silver halo, like a full moon, dominates his head and figure, and all but obliterates
the myriad flashings of the ethereal azures.   As
if on the edges of a second halo of larger radius,

the cerulean spaces are broken by thin lightning-like streaks of red and white flame, whose many serpent tongues are sucked to the centre as if on the breath of a cyclone. But the dominating, mystical feature is the system of intertwisted magnetic rays that i sues from the top of the Rakan's head, at first a slender spiral of white fire, curling as smoke from censer, but shortly expanding into an unresolvable tangle, whence radiate three larger, undulating rays, as if of magnetic communication with the cardinal points of space. A third eye set vertical in the forehead proves a Buddha's transcendent intelligence. The dark brown and gold of his superbly pyramidally-arranged robe strike a wonderful, solemn chord with the red and blue fires, and contrast with the gorgeous coloring of the terrestrial garments below, in which blues shot with red still predominate. One must say that in the whole range of imaginative celestial conception in Western art, whether in the mediæval transports of Fra Angelico's saints or in the cruder, if more intense, apocalyptic visions of William Blake, there has been realized nothing comparable to this transcendent creation.

21. This noble conception carries us into a sphere where comparison is challenged with Dante. The descent of these gracious figures through a hopeless gloom of rock, and icy fall, and trees of uncanny foliage, — as if they were dropping from one cloud terrace to another, the edges of the lowest holding back the sinking mass like the prows of ships, — is for the purpose of throwing alms to a

crowd of ragged outcasts beneath, whether spirits from one of torture's many cells, or lepers banished to this desolate spot, — outcasts who, flinging aside their meagre loads, fight like demons for the boon. Though the splendidly disposed robes of the Rakan are not drawn in Ririomin's style with firm swelling stroke, yet the broken nervousness of this artist's touch has enabled him to render the squalid rags and emaciated limbs with an intensity that nothing in early Italian frescos equals.

22. If the delicate tones of this picture had been more perfectly preserved it would probably rival in unearthly beauty No. 20. It represents similarly the transfiguration of a saint, who in this case stands erect in attitude of prayer above a rosy cloud. From his whole body, and especially from his halo, radiate masses of undulating blue rays, across whose magnetic torrent fall celestial flowers from the hands of angels floating in its upper spaces. Between the groups of the Rakan standing on earth a Deva in a puff of cloud emerges from below bearing in his hands a large golden dish, whose thin flames seem to lend potency to the miracle. This picture has been in places retouched, and the stained halo has lost its luminosity.

23. Here four Rakan pray about a large bell-gong which a servant strikes. The fifth saint sits on a rock above, hooded in his stole, in utter trance, and backed by a ghostly dawning halo from behind, which emerges a splendid Deva king, his

blade tipped with an enormous jewel, crossed upon his arms, his fingers locked in a special sacred symbol. Leafy creepers and tangled vines hang from the upper rocks in a style recalling secular work of later Sung. The drapery is firmly executed and is specially fine in the simple catenary curves of the tranced figure, which has served as model to more than one Takuma master in Japan.

24. The Rakan descend on folds of yellow sulphurous cloud, self-luminous, brightening the gloom of the lowest hell, of which a glimpse is seen beneath in the mountain sown with sword blades, and in the cauldron where the souls of the damned are eternally boiling. But, through the intervention of these saviors, a miracle has taken place. The very flames that leap about the horrid vessel are beaten down; the steaming water has been cooled into a sweet lake, from which spring, by divine grace, lotus plants with blossoms of blue, red, and white. The agonized souls turn in an ecstasy of relief toward the Rakan, or, as if half crazed, laugh at their unlooked-for reprieve. The very cow-headed fiend, who, with a trident has prevented their escape, is forced to his knees; his hands clutch as if in the inchoate action of unwonted prayer; and the head rolls upward in the attitude of a stricken beast.

25. This picture is dominated by the force of motion in the Niagara-like cataract across which the Rakan walk. A corresponding torrent in the air makes itself felt in the swing of their garments, and in

the wrenching of the tree branches above. Again, the almost horizontal lines of the water above the upper and lower falls are repeated sympathetically in the splendid spread of the two straw hats. The head, hat, and shoulders of the upper figure in blue have much of Ririomin's finest dignity. The attitude of the elemental, who, without possessing the spiritual power which would enable him to float upon the surface, yet plunges boldly in trusting to the sacred rolls he carries, intensifies the feeling of dizzy flow in the water.

26. Here is a large, strong rendering of the architecture of a Chinese Buddhist temple, whose rectangular spaces dominate the line and color composition. The foremost building is apparently the library, where sacred scrolls are kept boxed on the shelves. The boxes are apparently brought in by the Rakan from a distance, as in some important act requiring the mystic intervention of a Deva, whether the enrichment of a new edifice or the magical transportation of scriptural treasures from distant lands. The soft color of the Rakan's gowns contrasts, as of something transcendent, with the hard reds of the pillars; and both are thrown back into atmosphere by the fine, dark mass of the temple tree, whose color is echoed in the gray of the tiled roofs. Especially fine is the tip of the small cryptomeria, which rises against the green wall of the farther court. The architectural detail of bracket and carved interspace is essentially that of Japanese temples, though the proportions differ.

27. In this the composition and color are grand, with the sweep of the double waterfall cut by the dragon-like branch, and by the rich procession of figures along the chasm's brink, below which emerge, from the whirlpool under the fall and amid spray transformed to mystic cloud, the figures of a water king, and of a blue elemental attendant who bears aloft the former's ruby banner.

28. The Rakan are engaged in the occupations of sewing and mending. They sit on soft, straw mats, threading a needle, ready with a pair of shears, embroidering colored garments with black or with white thread. A servant comes in at the back bringing utensils for tea. Palmetto trees spread their delicate fan-like fingers. The composition is strengthened by their stems, and by the fence-rails made from their wood. The preservation of the color is remarkable, especially of the cloud pattern in the dress of the foremost Rakan, and in the reds and browns of the standing boy.

29. Sitting on green Buddhist chairs are four Rakan, finely draped in rich, pearly robes. From behind, through an avenue of gnarled trunks, the fifth Rakan is borne in a black sedan chair upon the shoulders of four horned elementals, whose uncouth limbs are echoed in the knots of the trees. A small monkey-faced attendant looks up in surprise.

30. Here is another subject in which architecture dominates the composition. The Rakan seem to be taking possession of a temple to which they have

arrived from a distance, their attendants laden
with baggage. The absence of all ornament on
their simple gowns gives them much more the
appearance of mendicants than is usual, and calls
for another scheme of low-toned color. A small
boy beats a drum in the temple yard in apparent
unconsciousness of this invasion, which we may
thus suppose invisible to ordinary mortals.

31. Before the injury to the upper portion, this must
have been one of the most impressive of the
series. The brilliancy of the simply disposed
Rakan group at night reading by candle light
from holy scripture, contrasted with the gloom
beyond the line of railing, — a gloom filled with
infinity of fine detail, — is almost Rembrandtesque
in its *notan* tone. The grim array of the spirit-
world, souls of kings, Deva, Bodhisattwa, and behind them the pale green and red features of
elementals, flocking to listen through the tangled
vine beclambered trunks of writhing trees, whose
knots and bone-like parasites peer out as an army
of skeletons, presents one of the weirdest feats of
imagination in all art.

32. The lower half of this picture contains the incident
of interest. The fifth Rakan, with the help of the
Deva on the left, brings to a couple standing on
earth, a little, seated, naked babe in the attitude
of prayer, held in a transparent, ruby globe, upon
a golden disk, by a female spirit dressed like a
Chinese nurse. This is probably the beautiful
suggestion of the conception of some future great
priest. In his left hand, the Rakan holds a cup

of holy water, with a willow spray for sprinkler. The naïve, sweetly expectant attitude of the simply drawn Chinese parents, and the wonderfully lifelike rendering of the careful bending nurse, in her wadded white robe, are especially charming.

33. The inferior execution of the lower figures must not blind us to the beauty and the great interest of the upper portion, where from the fingers and thumb of the left hand of the central dignified Rakan we see issuing five separate, undulating lines of magnetic influence, finding their way through blue and cloudy space, doubtless to the planetary force-centres with which they are severally affiliated.

34. Though much defaced, this beautiful composition reveals the Rakan gazing across the rail of a temple terrace into a sacred lotus-pond, — such as is found in every Oriental monastery,— whence, in obedience to a boy's order, a Hindoo servant, waist deep in the water, culls the choicest blossoms. A figure behind, probably a priest of lower rank, arranges the flowers in a celadon vase. The easy disposition of the draperies and the boy's fine attitude are features; while the pink blossom held in the latter's hand, and not retouched, illustrates the beautiful drawing of petals. The panel decoration of fighting lions is much like. that found on the borders of some of Ririomin's costumes.

35. This is a representation of the tonsure of a chief Rakan. The lines are angular and awkward, but the colors fresh, and the heads and the poses naïve.

Artistically, the fine dark blue garden rock, combined with the rich browns of the bamboo fence, as also the contrast of these darks and of the dark boy with the mingled feathers of cloud and banana leaf, are the striking features.

36. In a rocky gorge cut by a tumbling brook, the Rakan are finishing their single daily repast. One holds in his hands a beautiful malachite bowl, now empty; another ties up a similar vessel in a white cloth; while the dominant figure reaches his upward with an arm magically extended, to catch a rill which leaps from out the dark rock-masses. The feeling of the artist, who, in concealing the unpleasant feature of this arm by covering it mostly with a sweeping red-brown cloud, is noticeable, as is also the low-toned harmony which this cloud makes with the blue-gray of the rocks.

37. Here is another instance of the Rakan travelling through the world to visit the central shrines of many countries. The door of this temple is ajar, and through the portal we see a corner of the golden altar with the colored lotus-throne of its Buddha. Four of the Rakan are supported by the cloud; the fifth steps upon the tiled floor of the gallery out of the hands of a Deva spirit who is literally realizing the Bible passage, " For he shall give his angels charge over thee." The drawing of the large banana plant in light green against the dark gray ground, is masterly.

38. If the colors of the Rakan were here better preserved, we should have one of the finest presentations of the Oriental method of throwing up

bright figures against an ink landscape. Yet the very blur of the low-toned robes adds to the mysterious effect of the thick grove, through whose leafless branches light shimmers, and across which flies upward from the outstretched blue bowl a cloud of light white flakes: or is it that an early snow in the chill December glen is being magically caught, and so annihilated, in the sacred receptacle?

39. The Rakan are multiplying copies of the Buddhist records. From their attitude of discussion, and the fact that the chief in full canonicals presides before an altar with incense, this may be the first transcription of legend or of lesson held in the memory of their personal experience. An interesting feature is the three-fold screen behind the master painted with ink landscapes on a white ground in the style of the famous Sung artist Kakki. The female figures above are beings from heaven expressing interest in the work, who probably aid in the interpretation.

40. Though the lower portion is cracked by time and broken by the unquiet jewel-like spots of the adoring figures, yet the upper group of the Rakan in the cloud is one of the most dignified in drapery-line, and in the simple unadorned color masses. Each head, too, is a fine study.

41. Rakan crossing the sea upon the backs of marine monsters, whose drawing makes the picture specially interesting. Three of them are clearly visible: one a fine turtle executed in ink; one a

mass of red and yellow jelly with a head slug-like, though giving the impression of a dragon's features; that in the foreground, a splendid specimen in full color of the dragon-like dolphin which so often appears in Buddhist literature, and is the tenth sign of the zodiac; a full moon shines clear above the high horizon.

42. An incantation scene upon a terraced floor. In the foreground a king with golden censer shrinks from the apparition of the holy spirits whom he has invoked, and who step from a cloud upon a cloth of white brocade held up for their feet by two Chinese ladies but dimly cognizant of the phenomenon. The way in which the mingled cloud and wave of their mystic journey blot out the solid tiles of the pavement is a magnificent rendering of the transition from the outer to the inner vision.

43. The noble dragon-like spiral which mediates this composition is defeated by a lack of clear *notan*, or dark and light arrangement. Its feature is the manifestation of elemental powers in storm, whose mists, unlike the outlined lapping of previous clouds, is executed in blended ink masses like those of secular painting. Out of the cloud's frothy portion pours the bulk of a colored dragon, elemental incarnation of the motions of water. In the blackest hollow are revealed the paraphernalia of electric storm, the bow of linked drums with flaming vases tied into the knots between each pair. A servant with mallets, unlike the extravagant Japanese Raiden, is swept into the vortex. Another with metal rattles seems impressed by

the dragon. Two superior spirits emerge from
the cloud, while, still nearer, the king of the storm
bows in obeisance to the will of the Rakan.

44. The interest here lies in the saint with flaming halo,
who falls rapidly through space, eyes opening in
his outstretched palms, and followed in a serpentine magnetic wake that reaches back to the very
moon by a graceful female figure in white with
two attendants. One feels that some gentle lunar
soul is being designedly brought down to earth by
the priestly messenger. Here is the only case in
which the line of magnetic attachment we have so
often noted is visibly connected with an orb.

CPSIA information can be obtained
at www.ICGtesting.com
Printed in the USA
LVIC06n1418050418
572434LV00013B/148